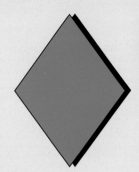

Diamond
Downhill

written by **Molly Dingles**

illustrated by **Len Dobson**

WASHINGTON SCHOOL
122 S Garfield Avenue
Mundelein, IL 60060

dingles & company   New Jersey

For Auntie Antionette

First printing

PUBLISHED BY dingles&company

P.O. Box 508 • Sea Girt, New Jersey • 08750
WEBSITE: www.dingles.com • E-MAIL: info@dingles.com

LIBRARY OF CONGRESS CATALOG CARD NO.: 2004095738
ISBN: 1-59646-043-1

Printed in the United States of America

ART DIRECTION & DESIGN BY Barbie Lambert
EDITED BY Andrea Curley
EDUCATIONAL CONSULTANT Maura Ruane McKenna
ART ASSISTANT Erin Collity
PRE-PRESS BY Pixel Graphics

Molly Dingles is the author of *Jinka Jinka Jelly Bean* and *Little Lee Lee's Birthday Bang*, as well as the Community of Color and the Community of Counting series. She is a writer and lyricist who holds a bachelor's degree in fine arts/theater from Mount Saint Mary's College and a master's degree in educational theater from New York University. She lives in Manasquan, New Jersey, with her husband, David.

Len Dobson is a graphic designer and illustrator. He has a national degree in graphic design from Guildford School of Art. His interest in children's books stems from the ten years he worked with BBC Worldwide and Warner Bros. to create cartoon characters for merchandising in the gift industry. Len has enjoyed a good deal of success in his professional career, and has since pursued his ambitions in publishing.

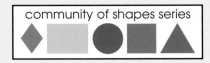
The Community of Shapes series is more than just a series of books about shape identification. The series demonstrates how individual people, places, and things combine to form a community. It allows children to view the world in segments and then experience the wonderment and value of the community as a whole.

What is a Diamond?

Technical definition:

A figure that has four equal straight lines and has two opposite acute angles and two opposite obtuse angles.

Kid-friendly definition:

A shape with four equal sides that stands on a point.

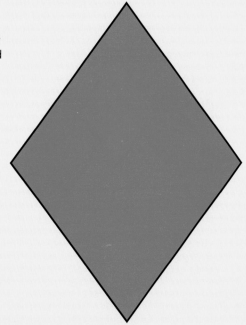

Diamonds
on a snowboard

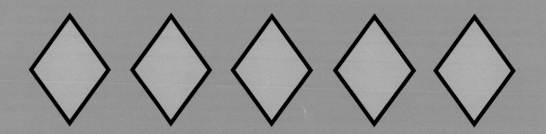

Diamond links
on the gates

Diamond lift tickets

Diamond hooks
for hanging skates.

Diamonds
on a sweater

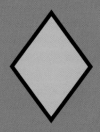

Diamond shape
on a hat

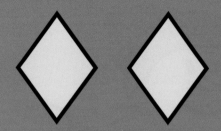

Diamonds on the cups

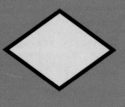

Diamond
name tag on a cat.

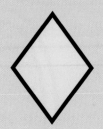

Diamond shapes
on shutters

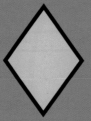

Diamond sign
on the slopes

Diamond
fishing hole

Diamond patterns on the ropes.

Diamond shapes are all around.

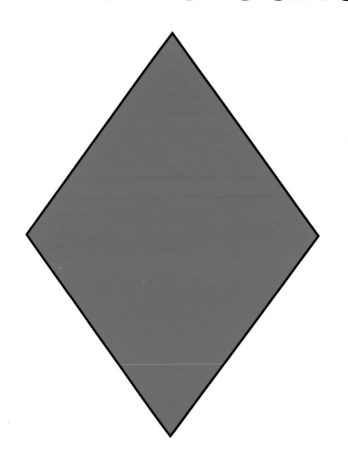

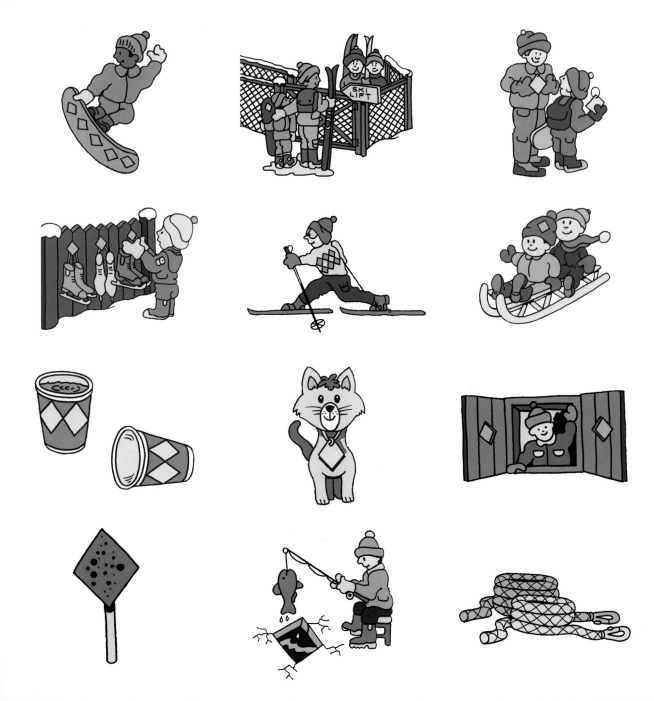

ABOUT SHAPES

Use the Community of Shapes series to teach your child to identify the most basic shapes and to help him or her relate these shapes to objects in the real world. ASK:

- What shape is this book about?
- Can you count the number of diamonds on the snowboard?
- Can you find all of the diamonds in the picture of the ski lodge?
- What is your favorite diamond-shaped object? Why?

ABOUT COMMUNITY

Use the Community of Shapes series to teach your child how he or she is an important part of the community. EXPLAIN TO YOUR CHILD WHAT A COMMUNITY IS.

- A community is a place where people live, work, and play together.
- Your family is a community.
- Your school is a community.
- Your neighborhood is a community.
- The world is one big community.

Everyone plays an important part in making a community work – moms, dads, boys, girls, police officers, firefighters, teachers, mail carriers, garbage collectors, store clerks, and even animals are all important parts of a community. USE THESE QUESTIONS TO FURTHER THE CONVERSATION:

- How are the children interacting with one another at the ski lodge?
- How are the people different from one another? How are they the same?
- What do they have in common?
- How is the community you see in this book like your community? How is it different?
- Describe your community.

OBSERVATIONS

The Community of Shapes series can be used to sharpen your child's awareness of the shapes of objects in their surroundings. Encourage your child to look around and tell you what he or she sees. ASK:

- Can you find diamond shapes in and around your house?
- What diamond-shaped object do you use most often?
- What kind of things could you use to make diamond shapes?

TRY SOMETHING NEW ... If you live in a part of the country where it snows, perhaps you can shovel an elderly neighbor's sidewalk and steps the next time it snows!

community of shapes series